BRAIN
FART

Running Press
Hachette Book Group
1290 Avenue of the Americas, New York, NY 10104
www.runningpress.com
@Running_Press

First Edition: April 2018

Published by Running Press, an imprint of Perseus Books, LLC, a subsidiary of Hachette Book Group, Inc.

The publisher is not responsible for websites (or their content) th are not owned by the publisher.

ISBN: 978-0-7624-6378-7

We all have those moments.

Sometimes you have a rough day and just want wind down and sit on the . . . uh, you know. The . . . thing. It's aargh, what's that word for that?

It's on the tip of your tongue, and you *know* you've said it before. A million times. It was a vocab word in second grade, for goodness' sakes.

Time is ticking. You still can't think of the word you need. You need to save face, for others and for yourself. So you use, uh, other words that are rattling around in your brain—those that just happen to be more readily accessible—and decide to dub the thing you're referring to as the "long-sleeve chair."

It's not just you. It's super common and is colloquially known as a *brain fart.*

That's why we've provided you with a little bit of science to explain this strange linguistic phenomenon, a few tips on overcoming it, and a handful of examples of pure cranial flatulence.

Couch! That was the word, *couch.*

Sigh.

So, Is There an Explanation for Brain Farts?

Though you may feel like a total dope in the moment, science says there's a reason for your brain breaking wind.

There are many scientists who study the relation between psychiatry and aging and "cognitive lapses," which is a fancy, sciency word for brain farts. There's no solid theory that everyone universally agrees on, but there are ideas. And there's historical precedent for the wacky ways we try to cope, too.

The Icelandic people have a concept called *kenning*, which is strongly associated with Old Norse poetry, like when they'd use the phrase "wave horse" for the word "ship" or "sky candle" for "sun." Plus, there's actually a language disorder known as anomic aphasia (also known as dysnomia), which is a situation where an individual has word retrieval failures and cannot express the words they want to say.

But most of us don't actually have a clinical disorder or happen to be an Old Norse poet. We just struggle sometimes with *imminent recall*. It's when you just know that what you

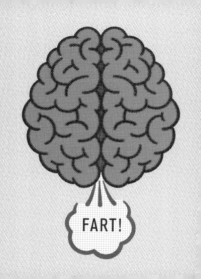

want to say is in there somewhere, and that's what creates that tip-of-the-tongue phenomenon. Lots of scientists believe that your memory's "retrieval process" sometimes breaks down, especially when your brain is distracted. Anything that affects cognitive health—like distraction, but also sleep deprivation, alcohol, anxiety, and just plain getting older—can contribute to a greater likelihood of your gray matter passing gas.

Really, brain farts tend to increase anytime your body undergoes something that is mentally trying—you know, *stress*. So if you're finding yourself experiencing less-than-ideal mental recall, grab that stress ball and throttle it like the dickens a few dozen times.

If it's still not coming back to you, the way most people tend to work around their brain farts to still be able to communicate their idea is by using circumlocution, which is a type of speech that circles around a specific idea with multiple words. Rather than directly evoking the idea with fewer and apter words—which, duh, you brain can't recall in the moment—yo talk in circles around the specific idea, so that suddenly you find yourself trying to say "candy corn" by calling it "triangle three-colored halloween food" instead. The great part about language is that much of the time, whomever you're talking to probably understands what you mean, even if they think you're kind of a moron.

But really, we're all morons at some point in our lives, aren't we? So pick up your stress ball and smoosh, squish, and squeeze your way through some giggles at hilarious brain farts.

I FORGOT THE WORD FOR THAT

"Hand me some sneeze paper!"

"OK . . . here's a *tissue.*"

"I keep crying those sad drops."

"We sane people tend to call them *tears*."

"Can we put one of those Halloween melons on our porch?"

"Yeah, I bought a *pumpkin* at the store already, don't worry."

"I spent too much. I need to put myself on one of those money diets."

"I think you mean put yourself on a budget."

"Go set the table, and make sure you put down those dish mattresses."

"The dishes do rest nicely on these *placemats*."

"I'm going to go take my nephew to the water zoo."

"Have fun at the *aquarium*, you lunatic."

"If you're going to the bodega, can you grab me a coffee and a breakfast cupcake?"

"I assume you mean grab you a *muffin*?"

"I saw a Western movie the other night and the streets were filled with that circle hay."

"You mean that *tumbleweeds* were rolling?"

"Oooh, spaghetti and meatballs? Give me some of that pasta sugar to put on top."

"Never really heard *Parmesan* cheese called that, but I actually kinda like it."

"Take the roast out of the oven, but use a cooking mitten."

"I'm always careful to use a potholder."

"All those pigeons keep shedding their bird leaves all over the park."

"Feathers. They're called *feathers*."

"What time do you want me to drive you to the plane station?"

"I can get myself to the *airport*, thanks."

"Did you close the door to the car house?"

"Uh huh, the door to the *garage* is no longer open."

"Make sure you take your sunglasses off before you go through the drive hole."

"It's OK, the *tunnel* isn't that dark."

"Did you see the feathers on that that gorgeous rainbow turkey?!"

"Yep, that peacock sure is pretty."

"My feet are cold—I gotta go put on some foot gloves."

"You can probably find them in the *sock drawer.*"

"I drank too much soda, and I can't stop mouth farting."

"I take it you're burping a lot?"

How to Get Rid of Brain Farts

When you're in the midst of a brain fart and that elusive word is just on the tip of your tongue, try to remember all of the words you to remember and associate with the missing word. Define it.

Does the word have a certain rhythm or feel that you can remember? Can you recall that pattern?

Focus on what you're trying to name. Visualize it. Now focus your attention on everything you remember and associate with it. Create a story in your mind about it. Working with a nice pile of synonyms can sometimes get you to where you want to be, though it sometimes just results in the colorful kinds of brain fart expressions we've included in this book.

If you can't get to that $1,000 word, don't sweat it. Just revel in your creation of a new phrase or the ridiculousness of your substitution. Maybe you could submit it to a dictionary. Or make a meme.

So don't forget: Keep yourself healthy, remember your synonyms, feel free to have a chuckle at your own expense, and make sure you squeeze the, uh . . . the rounded moosh sphere. You know. That thing.

This book has been bound using handcraft methods and Smyth-sewn to ensure durability.

The cover and interior were designed by Josh McDonnell.

The text was written by Sarah Royal.